Saint Croix National Scenic Riverway

Acoustical Monitoring 2011

Natural Resource Technical Report NPS/NRSS/NRTR—2012/544

Emma Lynch
National Park Service
Natural Sounds and Night Skies Division
1201 Oakridge Drive, Suite 100
Fort Collins, CO 80525

February 2012

U.S. Department of the Interior
National Park Service
Natural Resource Stewardship and Science
Fort Collins, Colorado

The National Park Service, Natural Resource Stewardship and Science office in Fort Collins, Colorado publishes a range of reports that address natural resource topics of interest and applicability to a broad audience in the National Park Service and others in natural resource management, including scientists, conservation and environmental constituencies, and the public.

The Natural Resource Technical Report Series is used to disseminate results of scientific studies in the physical, biological, and social sciences for both the advancement of science and the achievement of the National Park Service mission. The series provides contributors with a forum for displaying comprehensive data that are often deleted from journals because of page limitations.

All manuscripts in the series receive the appropriate level of peer review to ensure that the information is scientifically credible, technically accurate, appropriately written for the intended audience, and designed and published in a professional manner.

Data in this report were collected and analyzed using methods based on established, peer-reviewed protocols and were analyzed and interpreted within the guidelines of the protocols.

Views, statements, findings, conclusions, recommendations, and data in this report do not necessarily reflect views and policies of the National Park Service, U.S. Department of the Interior. Mention of trade names or commercial products does not constitute endorsement or recommendation for use by the U.S. Government.

This report is available from the Natural Sounds and Night Skies Division website (http://www.nature.nps.gov/naturalsounds/) and the Natural Resource Publications Management website (http://www.nature.nps.gov/publications/nrpm/).

Please cite this publication as:

Lynch, E. 2012. Saint Croix National Scenic Riverway: Acoustical monitoring 2011. Natural Resource Technical Report NPS/NRSS/NRTR—2012/544. National Park Service, Fort Collins, Colorado.

NPS 630/112757, February 2012

Contents

Tables

Figures

Executive Summary

In 2011, one acoustical monitoring system was deployed at Saint Croix National Scenic Riverway (SACN) for 34 days. The purpose of this monitoring effort was to characterize existing sound levels and estimate natural ambient sound levels as well as identify audible sound sources prior to the proposed re-opening of the Zavoral Gravel Mine in Scandia, Minnesota. At the time that this report was written, an EIS was being prepared for the reopening of the gravel mine, as required under the State of Minnesota Rules of decision-making.

For the purposes of this document, we will refer to "noise" as any human-caused sound that masks or degrades natural sounds (Lynch et al. 2011). Sources of noise at SACN include vehicle noise from nearby roads, boat traffic, and aircraft. Table 1 displays percent time audible values for each of these common noise sources during the monitoring period as well as ambient sound levels. A number of biologic sounds were also present during the monitoring period. Song birds and wind through vegetation were particularly prominent sound sources, but coyotes (*Canis latrans*), gray tree frogs (*Hyla versicolor*), green frogs (*Rana clamitans*), and barred owls (*Strix varia*) also appeared with regularity. Ambient sound pressure levels were measured continuously over the 34 day monitoring period by a calibrated, Type 1, Larson Davis 831 sound level meter. Percent time audible metrics were calculated by a trained technician after monitoring was complete. See Methods section for protocol details and equipment specifications.

Table 1. Mean percent time audible for all extrinsic sounds, aircraft, watercraft, and vehicles

| Site ID | Site Description | Mean percent time audible | | | | Median Existing Ambient (L_{50}) in dBA | | Median Natural Ambient (L_{nat}) in dBA | |
		All Extrinsic	Aircraft	Watercraft	Vehicles	Day	Night	Day	Night
SACN001	Swing Bridge Island	56.06	13.72	10.03	16.91	39.4	29.80	35.10	26.60

In determining the current conditions of an acoustical environment, it is informative to examine how often sound pressure levels exceed certain values. Table 2 reports the percent of time that measured levels were above four key values. The first value, 35 dBA, is designed to address the health effects of sleep interruption. Recent studies suggest that sound events as low as 35 dB can have adverse effects on blood pressure while sleeping (Haralabidis, 2008). The second value addresses the World Health Organization's recommendations that noise levels inside bedrooms remain below 45 dBA (Berglund et al., 1999). The third value, 52 dBA, is based on the EPA's speech interference level for speaking in a raised voice to an audience at 10 meters. This value addresses the effects of sound on interpretive presentations in parks. The final value, 60 dBA, provides a basis for estimating impacts on normal voice communications at 1 meter. Kayakers, hikers, or visitors viewing scenic areas in the park would likely be conducting such conversations.

Table 2. Percent time above metrics

| Site ID | % Time above sound level: 0700 to 1900 (Day) | | | | % Time above sound level: 1900 to 0700 (Night) | | | |
	35 dBA	45 dBA	52 dBA	60 dBA	35 dBA	45 dBA	52 dBA	60 dBA
SACN001	79.4	24.7	9.96	2.63	30.65	10.94	4.57	1.32

Introduction

A 1998 survey of the American public revealed that 72 percent of respondents thought that providing opportunities to experience natural quiet and the sounds of nature was a very important reason for having national parks, while another 23 percent thought that it was somewhat important (Haas & Wakefield 1998). In another survey specific to park visitors, 91 percent of respondents considered enjoyment of natural quiet and the sounds of nature as compelling reasons for visiting national parks (McDonald et. al 1995). Acoustical monitoring provides a scientific basis for assessing the current status of acoustic resources, identifying trends in resource conditions, quantifying impacts from other actions, assessing consistency with park management objectives and standards, and informing management decisions regarding desired future conditions.

National Park Service Natural Sounds and Night Skies Division

The Natural Sounds and Night Skies Division (NSNSD) helps parks manage sounds in a way that balances access to the park with the expectations of park visitors and the protection of park resources. The NSNSD addresses acoustical issues raised by Congress, NPS Management Policies, and NPS Director's Orders. The NSNSD works to protect, maintain, or restore acoustical environments throughout the National Park System. Its goal is to provide coordination, guidance, and a consistent approach to soundscape protection with respect to park resources and visitor use. The program also provides technical assistance to parks in the form of acoustical monitoring, data processing, park planning support, and comparative analyses of acoustical environments.

Soundscape Planning Authorities

The National Park Service Organic Act of 1916 states that the purpose of national parks is "... to conserve the scenery and the natural and historic objects and the wild life therein and to provide for the enjoyment of the same in such manner and by such means as will leave them unimpaired for the enjoyment of future generations." In addition to the NPS Organic Act, the Redwoods Act of 1978 affirmed that, "the protection, management, and administration of these areas shall be conducted in light of the high value and integrity of the National Park System and shall not be exercised in derogation of the values and purposes for which these various areas have been established, except as may have been or shall be directly and specifically provided by Congress."

Direction for management of natural soundscapes[1] is represented in 2006 Management Policy 4.9:

> The Service will restore to the natural condition wherever possible those park soundscapes that have become degraded by unnatural sounds (noise), and will protect natural soundscapes from unacceptable impacts. Using appropriate management planning, superintendents will identify what levels and types of unnatural sound constitute acceptable impacts on park natural soundscapes. The frequencies, magnitudes, and durations of acceptable levels of unnatural sound will vary throughout a park, being generally greater in developed areas. In and adjacent to parks, the Service will monitor

---

[1] The 2006 Management Policy 4.9 and related documents refer to "soundscapes" instead of "acoustic resources." When quoting from this authority, it is advisable to note that the term often refers to resources rather than visitor perceptions.

human activities that generate noise that adversely affects park soundscapes [acoustic resources], including noise caused by mechanical or electronic devices. The Service will take action to prevent or minimize all noise that through frequency, magnitude, or duration adversely affects the natural soundscape [acoustic resource] or other park resources or values, or that exceeds levels that have been identified through monitoring as being acceptable to or appropriate for visitor uses at the sites being monitored (NPS 2006a).

It should be noted that "the natural ambient sound level—that is, the environment of sound that exists in the absence of human-caused noise—is the baseline condition, and the standard against which current conditions in a soundscape [acoustic resource] will be measured and evaluated" (NPS 2006b). However, the desired acoustical condition may also depend upon the resources and the values of the park. For instance, "culturally appropriate sounds are important elements of the national park experience in many parks" (NPS 2006b). In this case, "the Service will preserve soundscape resources and values of the parks to the greatest extent possible to protect opportunities for appropriate transmission of cultural and historic sounds that are fundamental components of the purposes and values for which the parks were established" (NPS 2006b).

Study Area

Saint Croix National Scenic Riverway (SACN) was established to protect its natural, cultural, scenic, and recreational values for present and future generations. The park itself is a thin ribbon of protected land that includes the rivers and about ¼ mile of land on either side. Land within this strip is a combination of NPS, State and local government ownership and privately-owned lands over which the NPS has purchased easements. The 252 mile long Riverway runs through two states, 11 counties, 7 state parks, 3 state forests, county forests, and over 1500 parcels of private land. It is also designated as a National Wild and Scenic River. One acoustical monitoring station was deployed in SACN during June and July of 2011 for about 34 days. The site was selected because of its proximity to the proposed location of the Zavoral Gravel Mine, and because the vegetation and biologic activity near this site are representative of a large portion of the park. The park has plans to submit an SCC request for additional monitoring in 2013.

Table 3. Site Location

Site ID	Site Name	Dates Deployed	Vegetation	Elevation	Latitude	Longitude
SACN001	Swing Bridge Is.	6/22-7/27/2011	Deciduous forest, wetland	227 m	45.26050	-92.75419

Figure 1. Acoustical and meteorological monitoring station at SACN001, Swing Bridge Island.

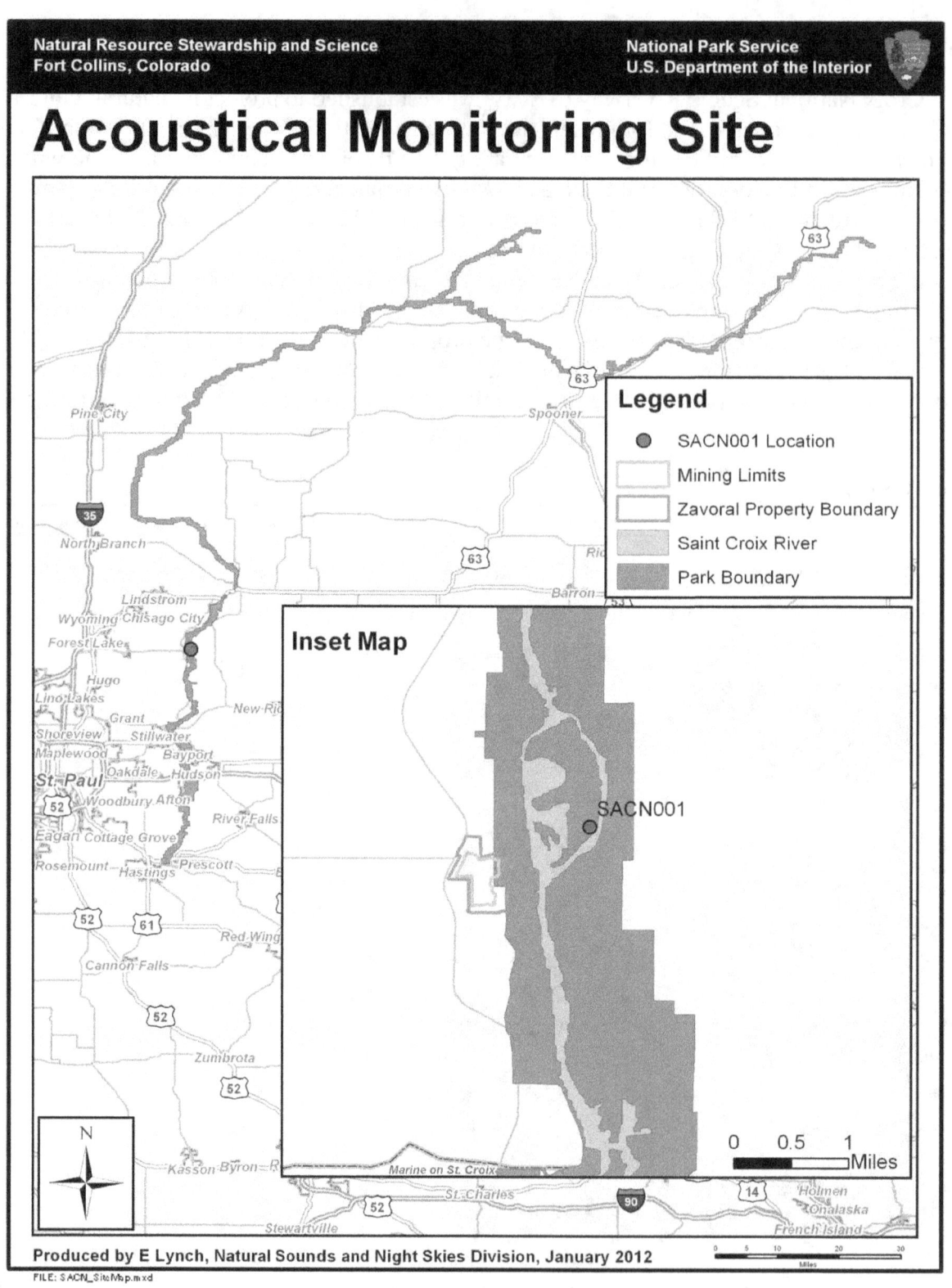

Figure 2. Location of monitoring site SACN001.

Methods

Automatic Monitoring

One Larson Davis 831 sound level meter (SLM) was employed over the thirty-four day monitoring period at SACN. The Larson Davis SLM is a hardware-based, real-time analyzer which constantly records one second sound pressure level (SPL) and 1/3 octave band data. This Larson Davis-based site met American National Standards Institute (ANSI) Type 1 standards. This sound level meter provided the information needed to calculate metrics described below in Calculation of Metrics.

The sampling station at SACN consisted of:

- Microphone with environmental shroud
- Preamplifier
- 8 12V LiMH rechargeable battery packs
- Anemometer (wind speed and direction)
- Temperature and humidity probe
- MP3 recorder

The sampling station collected:

- SPL data in the form of A-weighted decibel readings (dBA) every second
- Continuous digital audio recordings
- One third octave band data every second ranging from 12.5 Hz – 20,000 Hz
- Continuous meteorological data including wind speed, direction, temperature, and relative humidity

Calculation of Metrics

The current status of the acoustical environment can be characterized by spectral measurements, durations, and overall sound levels (intensities). The NSNSD uses descriptive figures and metrics to interpret these characteristics. Two fundamental descriptors are existing ambient (L_{50}) and natural ambient (L_{nat}) sound levels. These are both examples of exceedence levels, where each L_x value refers to the sound pressure levels that is exceeded x% of the time. The L_{50} represents the median sound pressure level, and is comprised of spectra (in dB) drawn from a full dataset (removing data with wind speed > 5m/s to eliminate error from microphone distortion.). The natural ambient (L_{nat}) is an estimate of what the ambient level for a site would be if all extrinsic or anthropogenic sources were removed. Unlike the existing ambient, the natural ambient is comprised of spectra drawn from a subset of the original data.

For a given hour (or other specified time period), L_{nat} is calculated to be the decibel level exceeded x percent of the time, where x is defined by equation (1):

$$x = \frac{100 - P_H}{2} + P_H , \qquad (1)$$

13

and P_H is the percentage of samples containing extrinsic or anthropogenic sounds for the hour. For example, if human caused sounds are present 30% of the hour, x = 65, and the L_{nat} is equal to the L_{65}, or the level exceeded 65% of the time. To summarize and display these data, the median of the hourly L_{nat} values for the daytime hours (0700-1900) and the median of the hourly L_{nat} values for the nighttime (1900-0700) are displayed in Figure 3 in the results section. Additionally, this figure separates the data into 33 one-third octave bands.

On-Site Listening

While the sound level meter provides information about how loud or quiet the acoustical environment is at a given time, we need .mp3 recordings or on-site listening sessions to know *what* or *who* is making the sound. On-site listening is the practice of placing an observer near the acoustical monitoring station with a handheld personal digital assistant (PDA). The observer listens for a designated period of time (in this case, one hour), and identifies all sound sources and their durations. On-site listening takes full advantage of human binaural hearing capabilities, and closely matches the experience of park visitors. Logistic constraints prevent comprehensive sampling by this technique, but selective samples of on-site listening provide a basis for relating the results of off-site listening to the probable auditory perception of events by park visitors and wildlife. On-site listening sessions are also an excellent screening tool for parks initiating acoustical environment studies. They produce an extensive inventory of sound sources, require little equipment or training, and can help educate park staff and volunteers.

Thus, two periods of on-site listening were conducted in order to discern the type, timing, and duration during sound-level data collection at SACN. As recommended by NSNSD protocol (NPS 2005) these sessions generally began at the top or middle of an hour and lasted for one hour. Staff recorded the beginning and ending times of all audible sound sources using custom-designed PDA software. These on-site listening sessions provided the basis for the calculation of metrics including the period of time between noise events (average noise free interval [NFI]), percent time each sound source was audible, and maximum, minimum, and mean length (in seconds) of sound source events. The results of these on-site listening sessions are summarized in Table 4.

Off-Site Listening/ Auditory Analysis

Auditory analysis was used to calculate the audibility of sound sources at SACN. Natural Sounds and Night Skies Division (NSNSD) staff analyzed a subset of .mp3 samples (10 seconds every two minutes for eight days of audio) in order to identify durations of audible sound sources. Staff used the total percent time extrinsic sounds were audible to calculate the natural ambient sound level for each hour (see Equation 1 below for more information). Bose Quiet Comfort Noise Canceling headphones were used for off-site audio playback to minimize limitations imposed by the office acoustic environment. For the complete results of this thorough audibility analysis, see Table 7 in the Off-Site Data Analysis section below.

Results

On-site Listening

Table 4 displays the results of the two on-site listening sessions. Each audible sound source is listed in the first column. Percent time audible, or PA, is the second column. The third column, Max Event, reports the maximum event length among the sessions for each sound source. Likewise, Mean Event and Min Event columns report the mean and minimum length of events, respectively. SD reports the standard deviation among event lengths, and the Count column reports the number of times that each sound source was audible. Max Event, Mean Event, Min Event, and SD Event are reported in seconds. The last row in the table, noise free interval (NFI), is a metric which describes the length of time between extrinsic or human-caused events (when only natural sounds were audible). NFI is also reported in seconds. These on-site listening tables are essentially a sound inventory of each site. They reveal the sounds one is likely to hear at or near this location.

Table 4. Summary of on-site audible sound sources for SACN001 n=2 hour-long sessions. Events are measured in minutes: seconds.

Sound Source Description	PA (%)	Max Event (mm:ss)	Mean Event (mm:ss)	Min Event (mm:ss)	SD Event (mm:ss)	Count (#)
Aircraft	0.0	0:02	0:02	0:02	0:01	1
Jet	17.0	2:30	1:05	0:06	0:43	19
Helicopter	4.0	2:05	1:35	0:48	0:41	3
Vehicle	81.0	24:40	3:27	0:03	6:03	28
Vehicle Door	0.0	0:02	0:02	0:02	0:01	1
Motorcycle	0.0	0:09	0:06	0:04	0:03	3
Watercraft	2.0	2:36	1:24	0:12	1:42	2
Grounds Care	6.0	6:35	3:24	0:12	4:31	2
Wind	0.0	0:04	0:04	0:04	0:01	1
Wind, Light	0.0	0:16	0:16	0:16	0:01	1
Bird	100.0	59:55	59:45	59:35	0:14	2
Insect	0.0	0:06	0:05	0:04	0:01	6
Natural Other	94.0	59:53	22:41	3:42	22:04	5
All Aircraft	21.2					
All Road Vehicles	80.7					
All Watercraft	2.3					
All Non-natural Sources	94.9					
All Natural Sources	99.6					
Noise Free Interval	5.1	1:04	0:22	0:01	0:21	17

The two sessions that informed this table were performed during daytime hours (2:25-3:25 pm and 3:00-4:00 pm) when human activity (particularly vehicle activity) was high. See the next section, Off-Site Data Analysis for results that summarize audibility over all hours of the day and night.

15

Off-Site Data Analysis

Metrics

In order to determine the effect that extrinsic noise audibility has on the acoustical environment, it is useful to examine the median hourly exceedence metrics. In Figure 3, the dB levels for 33 one-third octave band frequencies over the day and night periods are shown. High frequency sounds (a cricket chirping) and low frequency sounds (water flowing in a river) often occur simultaneously, so we split the frequency spectrum into 33 smaller ranges, each encompassing one-third of an octave. For each one-third octave band, dB level is recorded once per second for the duration of the monitoring period. Recording the sound intensity of each one-third octave band (combined with digital audio recordings) allows acoustic technicians to determine what types of sounds are contributing to the overall sound pressure level of a site. The grayed area of the graph represents sound levels outside of the typical range of human hearing. The exceedence levels (L_x) are also shown for each one-third octave band. They represent the dB exceeded x percent of the time. For example, L_{90} is the dB that has been exceeded 90% of the time, and only the quietest 10% of the samples can be found below this point. On the other hand, the L_{10} is the dB that has been exceeded 10% of the time, and 90% of the measurements are quieter than the L_{10}. The bold portion of the column represents the difference between L_{50} (existing ambient) and L_{nat} (natural ambient). The height of this bold portion is a measure of the contribution of anthropogenic noise to the existing ambient sound levels at this site. The size of this portion of the column is directly related to the percent time that human caused sounds are audible. When bold portions of the column do not appear the natural and existing ambient levels were either very close to each other, or were equal.

L_{nat} and L_{50} are bordered above by L_{10} and below by L_{90}, which essentially mark the median, maximum, and minimum sounds pressure levels over the 30 day monitoring period. The typical frequency levels for transportation, conversation and songbirds are presented on the figure as examples for interpretation of the data. These ranges are estimates and are not vehicle-, species, or habitat-specific. Notice in Figure 3 that contributions of songbirds are prominent in daytime hours, and that nighttime sound levels in the same frequencies are much quieter. In fact, in all frequencies, nighttime levels were quieter than daytime levels. This is a common occurrence in park settings.

It can be useful to review each one third octave band on these figures to predict the audibility of one sound or the masking of another. Notice that songbirds and transportation noise are audible at different frequency spectrums. There may be times when transportation sounds are louder than the songbirds. In this case, bird sounds would not be masked because their song is audible at a different frequency. If both of these sounds are within similar or overlapping frequency ranges, and one sound is louder than the other, then the quieter sound could be masked.

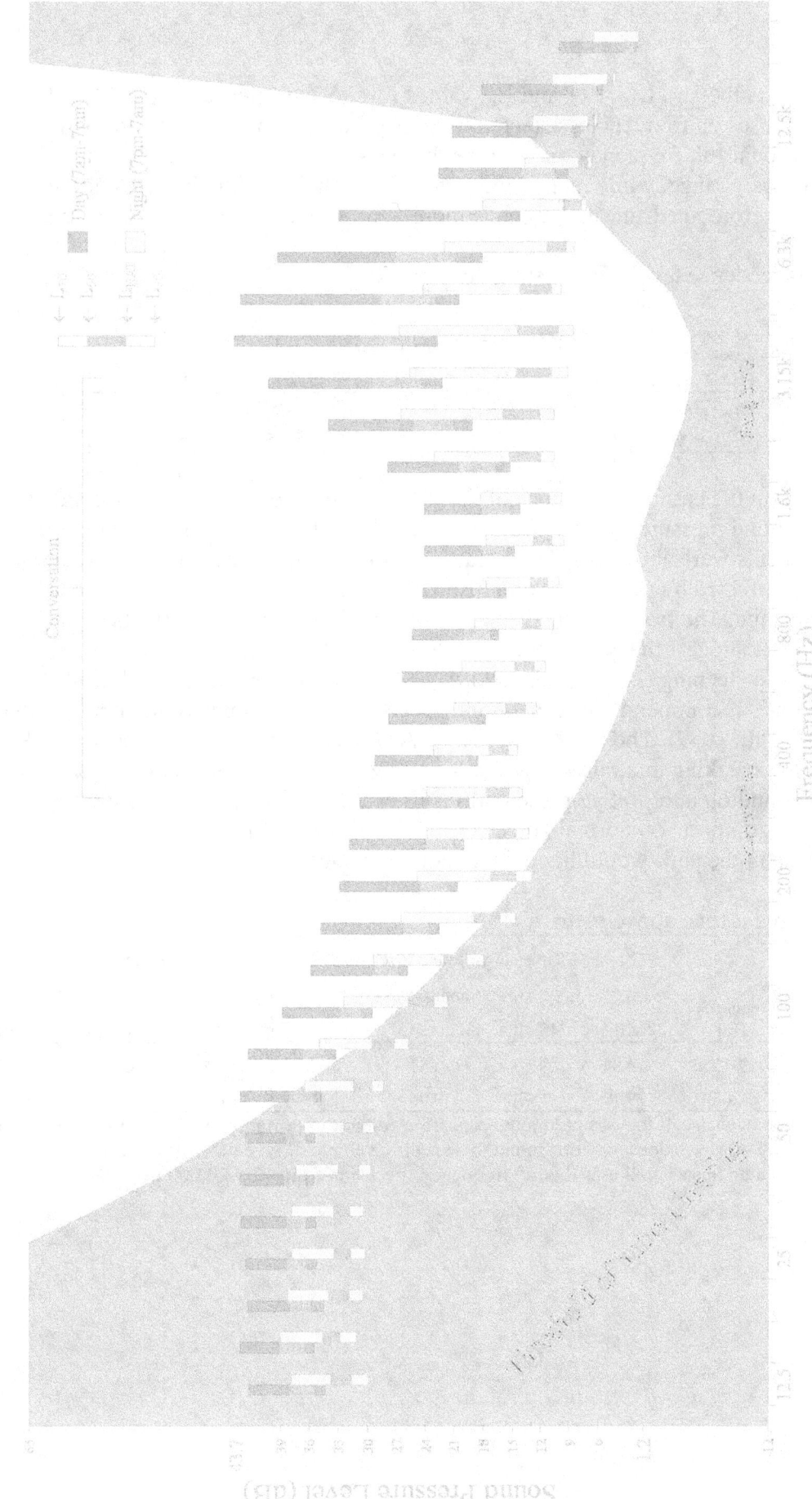

Figure 3. Day and night dB levels for 33 one-third octave bands at SACN001

17

Table 5 reports the L_{90}, L_{nat}, L_{50}, and L_{10} values for the sites measured at SACN. The top value in each cell focuses on frequencies affected by transportation noise whereas the lower values use the conventional full frequency range. Most human-caused noise is confined to the truncated, lower-frequency range, while many loud natural sounds, including insects and birds, are higher in pitch. Therefore, the truncated range is more appropriate for identifying noise levels in parks.

Table 5. Exceedence levels for existing conditions

Site	Frequency (Hz)	Exceedence levels (dBA): 0700 to 1900 hours (Day)				Exceedence levels (dBA): 1900 to 0700 hours (Night)			
		L_{90}	L_{nat}	L_{50}	L_{10}	L_{90}	L_{nat}	L_{50}	L_{10}
SACN001	20-1,250	26.0	26.9	29.2	35.5	20.4	21.5	23.6	28.5
	12.5-20,000	33.4	35.1	39.4	50.5	25.5	26.6	29.8	37.5

In determining the current conditions of an acoustical environment, it is important to examine how often sound pressure levels exceed certain values. Table 6 reports the percent of time that measured levels were above four key values. The top value in each split-cell focuses on frequencies affected by transportation noise whereas the lower values use the conventional full frequency range. The first, 35 dBA is designed to address the health effects of sleep interruption. Recent studies suggest that sound events as low as 35 dB can have adverse effects on blood pressure while sleeping (Haralabidis, 2008). The second value addresses the World Health Organization's recommendations that noise levels inside bedrooms remain below 45 dBA (Berglund et al., 1999). The third value, 52 dBA, is based on the EPA's speech interference threshold for speaking in a raised voice to an audience at 10 meters. This threshold addresses the effects of sound on interpretive presentations in parks. The final value, 60 dBA, provides a basis for estimating impacts on normal voice communications at 1 meter. Hikers and visitors viewing scenic vistas in the park would likely be conducting such conversations.

Table 6. Percent time above metrics

Site ID	Frequency (Hz)	% Time above sound level: 0700 to 1900 hours (Day)				% Time above sound level: 1900 to 0700 hours (Night)			
		35 dBA	45 dBA	52 dBA	60 dBA	35 dBA	45 dBA	52 dBA	60 dBA
SACN001	20-1250 [1]	13.84	1.83	0.31	0.03	5.37	0.64	0.13	0.02
	12.5-20,000 [2]	79.40	24.70	9.96	2.63	30.65	10.94	4.57	1.32

1. The top value in each cell focuses on frequencies affected by transportation, which approximately correspond to 20-1250 hertz. This range does not correspond to a specific vehicle or type of transportation.
2. The bottom value in each cell uses the full frequency spectrum, from 12.5-20,000 hertz.

Audibility

Audibility results are presented on the following pages. Table 7 shows the mean percentage of time that all noise sources were audible, based on eight days of auditory analysis. Figure 4, Figure 5, and Figure 6 show hourly audibility results and compare overall noise audibility to sources of interest: aircraft, vehicles, and watercraft, respectively. Interestingly, although vehicle activity is probably highest during the day near SACN001, listening results indicated the opposite. It is likely that the presence of other noise sources and/or biologic sounds in the same frequency range (watercraft, aircraft, or wind) during the midday hours masked the sound of passing vehicles. When the masking sources subsided in the early morning and evening hours, the acoustical monitoring system was able to detect vehicle noise.

Table 7. Mean hourly percent time audible for each noise source at SACN001

Noise source	00h	01h	02h	03h	04h	05h	06h	07h	08h	09h	10h	11h	12h	13h	14h	15h	16h	17h	18h	19h	20h	21h	22h	23h
Jet	1.2	2.5	3.3	4.2	7.1	3.3	3.8	18.8	7.1	9.2	18.8	10.8	4.6	13.3	12.1	13.8	15.8	8.7	5.8	23.7	11.3	4.2	11.7	3.3
Propeller	0.0	0.0	0.0	0.0	0.4	2.9	1.7	0.4	5.8	9.6	11.3	10.4	6.7	9.2	5.4	6.2	8.7	6.2	10.8	8.3	1.2	0.8	2.5	0.0
Helicopter	0.0	0.0	0.0	0.0	0.0	0.0	0.0	0.0	0.0	0.0	0.8	0.0	0.0	0.0	0.0	0.0	0.0	0.0	0.0	0.8	0.0	0.0	0.0	0.8
Vehicle, unknown	0.0	0.0	0.0	1.7	0.8	0.0	0.0	0.0	0.0	0.0	0.0	0.4	0.0	0.0	0.4	0.8	0.0	0.8	0.4	0.4	0.4	2.1	0.0	0.0
Automobile	37.1	29.2	18.8	23.3	32.1	18.3	30.4	28.7	17.9	8.3	4.2	7.9	7.1	6.2	6.2	5.4	3.8	3.3	6.2	7.1	10.4	18.8	14.6	25.0
Vehicle alarm, horn	0.0	0.0	0.0	0.0	0.0	0.0	0.0	0.0	0.4	0.4	0.0	0.0	2.9	9.6	2.9	0.0	0.0	0.0	0.0	0.0	0.0	0.0	0.0	0.0
Vehicle door	0.0	0.0	0.0	0.0	0.0	0.0	0.4	0.0	0.0	0.0	0.0	0.0	0.0	0.0	0.0	0.0	0.0	0.0	0.4	0.0	0.0	0.0	0.0	0.0
Motorcycle	0.0	0.0	0.0	0.0	0.0	0.8	0.0	0.4	0.0	0.4	0.0	0.0	0.0	0.0	0.4	0.8	0.4	0.8	0.4	0.8	0.0	1.2	0.0	0.4
Truck	0.0	0.0	1.2	0.0	0.0	0.0	0.0	0.4	0.0	0.0	0.0	0.0	0.0	0.0	0.4	0.4	0.0	0.0	0.0	0.0	0.0	0.0	0.0	0.8
Watercraft, unknown	0.0	0.8	2.9	0.4	1.2	7.9	3.8	8.7	12.5	8.7	17.1	15.8	13.3	13.8	17.5	12.9	8.3	22.1	20.0	19.6	17.5	11.3	2.1	2.1
Watercraft, non-motorized	0.0	0.0	0.0	0.0	0.0	0.0	0.0	0.0	0.0	0.0	0.0	0.0	0.0	0.4	0.0	0.0	0.0	0.0	0.0	0.0	0.0	0.0	0.0	0.0
Train	0.0	0.0	0.0	0.0	0.0	0.0	0.0	0.0	0.0	0.0	0.0	0.0	0.0	0.0	0.0	1.2	1.2	0.0	0.0	0.0	0.0	0.0	0.0	0.0
Train rumble	0.0	0.0	0.0	0.0	0.0	0.0	0.0	0.0	0.0	1.2	1.2	1.7	1.7	1.7	0.0	4.6	5.0	2.9	3.8	2.1	1.2	8.7	2.9	0.0
Train whistle	0.4	0.0	0.0	0.0	0.0	0.0	0.0	0.0	0.0	0.0	0.0	0.8	0.0	0.4	0.0	0.8	1.2	0.8	0.4	0.0	0.4	0.8	0.8	0.0
Generator	0.0	0.0	0.0	0.0	0.0	0.0	0.0	0.0	0.0	0.0	0.0	0.0	1.7	0.0	0.0	0.0	0.0	0.0	0.0	0.0	0.0	0.0	0.0	0.0
Grounds care	0.0	0.0	0.0	0.0	0.0	0.0	0.0	0.0	0.0	0.0	0.0	0.0	0.0	0.0	0.0	0.0	0.0	0.0	0.0	0.0	0.0	0.4	0.0	0.0
People	0.0	0.0	0.0	0.0	0.0	0.0	0.0	0.0	0.0	0.0	0.0	0.0	0.0	0.0	0.0	0.4	0.0	0.0	0.4	0.0	0.0	0.0	0.0	0.0
Voices	0.0	0.0	0.0	0.0	0.0	0.0	0.0	0.0	0.0	0.0	0.4	0.4	2.5	2.1	3.3	2.9	3.3	3.8	1.2	2.5	1.7	2.1	0.8	0.0
Portable audio devices	0.0	0.0	0.0	0.0	0.0	0.0	0.0	0.0	0.4	0.0	0.0	0.0	0.0	0.0	0.0	0.0	0.0	0.0	0.0	0.0	0.0	0.0	0.0	0.8
Fireworks	0.4	0.0	0.0	0.0	0.0	0.0	0.0	0.0	0.0	0.0	0.0	0.0	0.0	0.0	0.0	0.0	0.0	0.0	0.0	1.7	4.2	4.6	16.3	5.0
Domestic dog	1.7	0.4	2.9	0.4	0.0	0.4	0.4	0.0	0.0	0.0	1.2	0.0	0.0	0.0	0.0	0.0	0.4	0.0	0.0	0.0	0.8	0.0	1.7	2.5
Construction	0.0	0.0	0.0	0.0	0.0	0.0	0.0	0.0	0.0	0.0	0.0	0.8	0.0	0.8	2.5	4.6	2.1	2.5	0.0	0.0	0.8	0.0	0.0	0.0
Non-natural unknown	1.7	5.8	7.1	4.2	7.5	18.3	12.1	12.1	15.0	12.1	10.4	12.9	14.6	15.4	14.6	16.7	7.5	16.3	12.1	17.1	27.9	10.0	16.7	11.3
All noise sources	40.8	38.3	36.2	34.2	48.8	51.7	52.1	67.9	59.2	48.3	62.9	59.6	52.5	66.7	62.1	63.3	53.3	64.2	60.0	78.7	72.9	59.6	64.2	47.9

21

Figure 4. Comparison of hourly aircraft audibility and overall noise audibility at SACN001

23

Figure 5. Comparison of hourly vehicle audibility and overall noise audibility at SACN001

25

Figure 6. Comparison of hourly watercraft audibility and overall noise audibility at SACN001

27

Discussion

The purpose of this study was twofold: characterize existing sound levels and estimate natural ambient sound levels at one site in Saint Croix National Scenic Riverway, and identify audible sound sources prior to the proposed re-opening of the Zavoral Gravel Mine in Scandia, Minnesota. Monitoring results were intended to give the park baseline information as well as inform management decisions. Sound pressure level data, meteorological data, and continuous audio were collected. Data were gathered from one site on Swing Bridge Island for approximately 34 days. The acoustical monitoring station was located here because of its proximity to the Zavoral Mine site and because the vegetation and biologic activity was representative of the rest of the scenic riverway. The park has plans to submit an SCC request for additional monitoring in 2013.

NSNSD staff calculated that the natural ambient sound level at this site ranged between 39.4 dBA during the daytime and 26.6 dBA at night. For comparison, a comprehensive 1982 study of noise levels in residential areas found that nearly 87% of US residents were exposed to day-night sound levels over 55 dB (and an additional 53% was exposed to day-night sound levels over 60 dB)(EPA 1982). Therefore, our results imply that the natural ambient sound level during the monitoring period was considerably quieter than most residential areas. However, noise still exists in SACN's acoustical environment. A detailed analysis of audibility at this site found that the three major noise sources (aircraft, vehicles, and watercraft) contributed significant amounts of noise to the acoustical environment (ranging from 10 to 17% audibility overall). Trains were also audible, to a lesser degree. The remaining sources of noise were intermittent (dogs, construction, personal audio devices), and could be characterized as "seasonal." For instance, although NSNSD avoided analyzing the 4th of July, fireworks were noted up to a few weeks before and after the holiday.

In addition to the various noise sources at SACN, many natural sounds were also recorded. Birds, insects, and amphibian sounds were recorded each day. Thunderstorms rolled in. Something jumped out of the water near the microphone. A pair of barred owls called to each other late at night. The proverbial tree even fell in the forest. These are just a handful of the many sounds that contribute to the unique acoustical environment at Saint Croix National Scenic Riverway.

Literature Cited

Berglund, B., Lindvall, T. and Schwela, D.H (Eds.). 1999. HWO. Guidelines for community noise. World Health Organization, Geneva.

Environmental Protection Agency (1982) National Ambient Noise Survey. Office of Noise Abatement and Control, Washington, DC.

Haas, G.E., & Wakefield, T.J. 1998. National parks and the American public: A national public opinion survey on the national park system. Washington D.C. and Fort Collins, CO.: National Parks and Conservation Association and Colorado State University.

Haralabidis Alexandros S., et. al. 2008. "Acute effects of night-time noise exposure on blood pressure in populations living near airports" European Heart Journal Advance Access. Published online February 12, 2008.

Landon, D.M., Krauseman, P.R., Koenen, K.K.G., & Harris, L.K. 2003. Pronghorn use of areas with varying sound pressure levels. The Southwestern Naturalist 48:725-728.

Lynch, E., Joyce, D., and Fristrup, K. 2011. An assessment of noise audibility and sound levels in U.S. National Parks. Landscape Ecology 26: 1297-1309.

McDonald, C. D., Baumgarten, R. M., and Iachan, R. 1995. Aircraft management studies: National Park Service Visitors Survey. HMMH Report No. 290940.12; NPOA Report No. 94-2, National Park Service, U.S. Department of the Interior.

National Park Service. 2005. Acoustic and Soundscape Studies in National Parks: Draft. Fort Collins, CO: NPS Natural Sounds and Night Skies Division.

National Park Service. 2006a. Management Policy 4.9: Soundscape Management.

National Park Service. 2006b. Management Policy 8.2.3: Use of Motorized Equipment.

Glossary of Acoustical Terms

Acoustical Environment
The actual physical sound resources, regardless of audibility, at a particular location.

Amplitude
The instantaneous magnitude of an oscillating quantity such as sound pressure. The peak amplitude is the maximum value.

Audibility
The ability of animals with normal hearing, including humans, to hear a given sound. Audibility is affected by the hearing ability of the animal, the masking effects of other sound sources, and by the frequency content and amplitude of the sound.

dBA
A-weighted decibel. A-Weighted sum of sound energy across the range of human hearing. Humans do not hear well at very low or very high frequencies. Weighting adjusts for this.

Decibel
A logarithmic measure of acoustic or electrical signals. The formula for computing decibels is: 10(Log10(sound level/reference sound level)). 0 dB represents the lowest sound level that can be perceived by a human with healthy hearing. Conversational speech is about 65 dB.

Diel
A 24-hour period usually consisting of a day and the adjoining night.

Extrinsic Sound
Any sound not forming an essential part of the park unit, or a sound originating from outside the park boundary.

Frequency
The number of times per second that the sine wave of sound repeats itself. It can be expressed in cycles per second, or Hertz (Hz). Frequency equals Speed of Sound/ Wavelength.

Hearing Range (frequency)
By convention, an average, healthy, young person is said to hear frequencies from approximately 20Hz to 20000 Hz.

Hertz
A measure of frequency, or the number of pressure variations per second. A person with normal hearing can hear between 20 Hz and 20,000 Hz.

Human-Caused Sound
Noise. Any sound that is attributable to a human source.

Intrinsic sound

A sound which belongs to a park by its very nature, based on the park unit purposes, values, and establishing legislation. The term "intrinsic sounds" has replaced "natural sounds" in order to incorporate both cultural and historic sounds as part of the acoustic environment of a park.

Listening Horizon

The range or limit of one's hearing capabilities. Just as smog limits the visual horizon, so noise limits the acoustic horizon.

L_{eq}

Energy Equivalent Sound Level. The level of a constant sound over a specific time period that has the same sound energy as the actual (unsteady) sound over the same period.

L_x

A metric used to describe acoustic data. It represents the level of sound exceeded x percent of the time during the given measurement period.

Masking

The process by which the threshold of audibility for a sound is raised by the presence of another sound.

Noise-Free Interval

The period of time between noise events (not silence).

Noise

Sound which is unwanted, either because of its effects on humans, its effect on fatigue or malfunction of physical equipment, or its interference with the perception or detection of other sounds (Source: McGraw Hill Dictionary of Scientific and Technical Terms).

Off-site Listening

The systematic identification of sound sources using digital recordings previously collected in the field.

Sound Level Floor (Noise Floor)

The lowest amplitude measurable by sound monitoring equipment.

NPS 630/112757, February 2012